THE USBORNE
INTERNET-LINKED
LIBRARY OF SCIENCE
MATERIALS

The Web sites recommended in this book can be accessed via the Usborne Quicklinks Web site at www.usborne-quicklinks.com. Usborne Publishing has made every effort to ensure that material on the recommended sites is suitable for its intended purpose, and the sites are regularly reviewed by Usborne editors. However, the content of a Web site may change at any time, and Usborne Publishing is not responsible for the accuracy or suitability of the information on any Web site other than its own. We recommend that children are supervised while on the Internet, that they do not use Internet chat rooms, and that you use Internet filtering software to block unsuitable material.

First published in 2001 by Usborne Publishing Ltd,
Usborne House, 83-85 Saffron Hill, London EC1N 8RT, England.

www.usborne.com

Printed in Spain

THE USBORNE
INTERNET-LINKED
LIBRARY OF SCIENCE
MATERIALS

Alastair Smith, Phillip Clarke and Corinne Henderson

Designed by Ruth Russell, Jane Rigby,
Chloë Rafferty and Adam Constantine

Digital illustrations by Verinder Bhachu
Digital imagery by Joanne Kirkby

Edited by Laura Howell

Cover design: Nicola Butler

Consultants: Elaine Wilson and Mark Beard

Web site adviser: Lisa Watts
Editorial assistant: Valerie Modd

Managing designer: Ruth Russell
Managing editor: Judy Tatchell

INTERNET LINKS

Throughout this book we have recommended websites where you can find out more about materials. To visit the sites, go to the **Usborne Quicklinks Website** where you will find links to all the sites.

1. Go to **www.usborne-quicklinks.com**
2. Type the keywords for this book: **science materials**
3. Type the page number of the link you want to visit.
4. Click on the links to go to the recommended sites.

Here are some of the things you can do on the websites recommended in this book:
- Watch animations about atoms, molecules and the states of matter.
- Investigate fireworks online, play a fireworks game and try a quiz
- Take a tour of metals and minerals found around the home.
- Test different metals in a virtual lab and watch them corrode.

SITE AVAILABILITY

The links in Usborne Quicklinks are regularly reviewed and updated, but occasionally you may get a message that a site is unavailable. This might be temporary, so try again later, or even the next day. Websites do occasionally close down and when this happens, we will replace them with new links in Usborne Quicklinks. Sometimes we add extra links too, if we think they are useful. So when you visit Usborne Quicklinks, the links may be slightly different from those described in your book.

DOWNLOADABLE PICTURES

Pictures marked with a ★ in this book can be downloaded from the Usborne Quicklinks Website. These pictures are for personal use only and must not be used for commercial purposes.

SAFETY ON THE INTERNET

Ask your parent's or guardian's permission before you connect to the Internet and make sure you follow these simple rules:

- Never give out information about yourself, such as your real name, address, phone number or the name of your school.

- If a site asks you to log in or register by typing your name or email address, ask permission from an adult first.

WHAT YOU NEED

To visit the websites you need a computer with an Internet connection and a web browser (the software that lets you look at information from the Internet). Some sites need extra programs (plug-ins) to play sound or show videos or animations.

If you go to a site and do not have the necessary plug-in, a message will come up on the screen. There is usually a link to click on to download the plug-in. For more information about plug-ins, go to Usborne Quicklinks and click on "Net Help".

NOTES FOR PARENTS

The websites described in this book are regularly reviewed and the links in Usborne Quicklinks are updated. However, the content of a website may change at any time and Usborne Publishing is not responsible for the content on any website other than its own. We recommend that children are supervised while on the Internet, that they do not use Internet Chat Rooms, and that you use Internet filtering software to block unsuitable material. Please ensure that your children read and follow the safety guidelines printed above. For more information, see the "Net Help" area on the Usborne Quicklinks Website.

www.usborne-quicklinks.com

Go to Usborne Quicklinks and enter the keywords "science materials" for:

- direct links to all the websites in this book

- free downloadable pictures, which appear throughout this book marked with a ★ symbol

SEE FOR YOURSELF

The *See for yourself* boxes in this book contain experiments, activities or observations which we have tested. Some recommended websites also contain experiments, but we have not tested all of these. This book will be used by readers of different ages and abilities, so it is important that you do not tackle an experiment on your own, either from the book or the Web, that involves equipment that you do not normally use, such as a kitchen knife or cooker. Instead, ask an adult to help you.

CONTENTS

This metal was changed from a solid to a liquid by adding huge amounts of heat. In this form, it is described as molten.

MATERIALS

Everything in existence is made of tiny particles called atoms. Substances such as oxygen, which are made up of only one kind of atom, are called elements. Normally, atoms bond together to form groups called molecules, the smallest part of any material that can exist alone. In this book, you can learn about the chemistry of many different materials and the elements from which they are made.

Each of the 65 metals that exist naturally on Earth has different chemical properties. For instance, the iron in this picture, which appears blue, has reacted with oxygen in the air to form a flaky brown layer called rust. This process is known as corrosion.

ATOMIC STRUCTURE

Atoms are the tiny particles of which everything is made. It is impossible to imagine how small an atom is. A hundred million atoms side by side would measure only 1cm, and a sheet of paper, like the ones that make up this book, is probably a million atoms thick.

This diagram uses coloured balls to represent the parts of an atom and illustrate the relationships between them.

SUBATOMIC PARTICLES

Atoms are made of smaller particles called **subatomic particles**. In the middle of every atom is its **nucleus**. The nucleus contains two types of subatomic particles, called **protons** and **neutrons**.

Protons and neutrons form the nucleus of an atom.

Neutron

Proton

Subatomic particles of a third type, called **electrons**, move around the nucleus. The electrons exist at different energy levels, called **shells**, around the nucleus. Each shell can have up to a certain number of electrons. When it is full, a new shell is started.

Electron shells

Electron

Proton

Neutron

Scientists now think that protons and neutrons are made of even smaller subatomic particles, called **quarks**.

In the middle of the atom is the nucleus. It is made of protons (shown in pink) and neutrons (shown in purple).

Most of an atom consists of empty space between the particles.

Electrons are trapped by their attraction to protons, which are in the nucleus. They whizz around the nucleus at different levels, called shells.

The two electrons shown in green exist in the first shell of this atom. Those in blue are in the second shell.

ELECTRICAL CHARGES

The subatomic particles that make up an atom are held together by electrical charges. Particles with opposite electrical charges are attracted to one another.

The protons have a positive electrical charge and the electrons have a negative charge. Neutrons have no electrical charge, so they are neutral.

| Proton: positive electrical charge. | Electron: negative electrical charge. | Neutron: no electrical charge. |

An atom usually has an equal number of positively charged protons and negatively charged electrons. This makes the atom itself electrically neutral.

This atom is electrically neutral.

It has four protons.

It has four electrons.

Its three neutrons have no effect on its electrical charge.

Electron

★

REPRESENTING ATOMS

Although atoms are often represented by diagrams like the main picture, scientists now believe that the electrons are held in cloud-like regions around the nucleus, as in the **electron cloud model** below.

Electron cloud model

Electrons can be anywhere within their cloud, at any time. Sometimes they even move outside it.

ELECTRON DENSITY

In the picture below, different colours show different levels of density of electrons in a group of atoms. The turquoise areas show where the electrons are most dense.

This is a picture of what you might see through an extremely powerful microscope.

Internet links

Go to www.usborne-quicklinks.com for links to the following websites:

Website 1 Explore the structure of an atom and compare different atoms.

Website 2 Try some fun activities to find out more about atoms.

Website 3 Read a guide to atoms and subatomic particles.

Website 4 Information about electrons including their discovery and how they have affected our lives.

Website 5 Take a look inside a carbon atom.

ATOMIC NUMBER

Atoms of different substances have different numbers of protons in their nucleus. The number of protons in the nucleus is called the **atomic number**.

The atomic number of an atom indicates what substance it is.

An atom usually has an equal number of protons and electrons, so the atomic number also shows how many electrons it has.

This type of machine is called a **cyclotron**, a device which scientists use to break atoms apart. Machines like this have enabled research into the nature of atoms, and the particles of which they are made.

The nucleus of a carbon atom has six protons, so its atomic number is six.

The nucleus contains six protons and six neutrons, so its mass number is 12.

Proton

Neutron

The nucleus of a phosphorus atom has 15 protons, so its atomic number is 15.

The nucleus contains 15 protons and 16 neutrons, so its mass number is 31.

MASS NUMBER

The more protons and neutrons an atom has, the greater its mass (the measurement of the amount of matter in the atom). The total number of protons and neutrons in an atom is called its **mass number**.

Electrons are left out of the mass calculation as they add so little to the mass of an atom.

A machine called a **mass spectrometer** can be used to help identify atoms by sorting them by mass.

Cyclotrons are used in certain industries. Manufacturers use them to create particular types of plastics. In hospitals, they are used to create radioactive isotopes to treat cancer patients.

ISOTOPES

Most atoms exist in a number of different forms, called **isotopes**. Each form has the same number of protons and electrons, but a different number of neutrons. So all the isotopes of an atom have the same atomic number, but they have different mass numbers.

The mass number of the isotope of an atom is written beside its name. For instance, carbon-12 has six protons and six neutrons.

These examples show the three isotopes of carbon.
 Proton
Neutron

Carbon 12 has six neutrons and six protons.

Carbon 13 has six protons and seven neutrons.

Carbon 14 has six protons and eight neutrons.

Isotopes have different physical properties but their chemical properties are the same. Most of the atoms in an **element** (a substance made up of only one type of atom) are a single isotope, with small amounts of other isotopes.

ANCIENT IDEAS

The idea that everything in the universe is made up of atoms is not a new one. Philosophers in Ancient Greece, 2,500 years ago, believed that matter was made up of particles that could not be cut any smaller. The word "atom" comes from the Greek word *atomos*, which means "uncuttable".

The theories of Aristotle, an Ancient Greek philosopher, influenced scientists and their studies on atoms for centuries.

Aristotle (384-322BC)

ATOMIC THEORY

The term "atom" was first used by the British chemist, John Dalton, when he put forward his **atomic theory** in 1807.

Dalton suggested that all chemical elements were made of very small particles, called atoms, that did not break up when chemicals reacted. He thought that every chemical reaction was the result of atoms joining or separating. Dalton's atomic theory provided the basis for modern science.

John Dalton (1766-1844)

Dalton used symbols to represent one atom of each element or substance.

Examples of Dalton's symbols

Zinc   Mercury   Sulphur

EARLY MODELS

Early in the twentieth century, scientists began to make models of atoms.

Ernest Rutherford (1871-1937) showed electrons with a negative electric charge circling a positively charged nucleus.

Rutherford's model

Niels Bohr (1885-1962) showed a model with electrons following specific orbits. In 1932, James Chadwick (1891-1974) showed the nucleus made of particles called neutrons and protons.

This model of an atom, which is also shown larger on pages 8-9, is based on models by Rutherford, Bohr and Chadwick.

Internet links

Go to **www.usborne-quicklinks.com** for links to the following websites:

Website 1 An introduction to elements with information on elements as atoms.

Website 2 Build your own carbon atom and find out about famous scientists like Niels Bohr.

Website 3 Explore a particle accelerator laboratory, the European Organization for Nuclear Research (CERN).

MOLECULES

Atoms are rarely found on their own. They usually cling, or bond, together to form molecules or large lattice structures. A **molecule** is a group of atoms that are bonded together to form the smallest piece of a substance that normally exists on its own. Molecules are much too small to be seen with the naked eye.

SHELLS AND BONDING

Most atoms have several shells of electrons*. The first shell of an atom can hold two electrons. The second and third shells can hold eight, although some atoms can hold up to 18 electrons in their third shells. When a shell is full, the electrons start a new shell. An atom is particularly stable when it has a full outer shell of electrons.

An argon atom has three full shells of electrons. It is a stable atom.

A sodium atom is unstable. It has only one electron in its third shell.

Atoms bond together in order to become stable. They do this by sharing electrons, or by giving up or taking electrons from another atom in order to achieve a full, or fuller, outer shell. Two hydrogen atoms, for instance, bond together to make a hydrogen molecule. They share their electrons, giving each atom a full outer shell.

Two hydrogen atoms

Electrons

Hydrogen molecule

Each atom has a full shell of two electrons, so it is stable.

* Electrons, 8.

This is a model of a molecule of DNA, a complicated chemical compound found in the cells of all living things.

CHEMICAL FORMULAE

An atom's name can be shown by a symbol (its **chemical symbol**). This is usually the first letter or two of its name in English, Latin or Arabic.

O   The symbol for oxygen

Au   The symbol for gold, from the Latin word *aurum*

Fe   The symbol for iron, from the Latin word *ferrum*

K   The symbol for potassium, from the Arabic word *kalium*

A **chemical formula** shows the atoms of which a substance is made and in what proportions. For example, each molecule of carbon dioxide is made up of one atom of carbon and two atoms of oxygen, so the formula for carbon dioxide is CO_2. The figure "2" shows the number of oxygen atoms in the molecule.

Molecule of carbon dioxide (CO_2)

- Oxygen atom
- Carbon atom
- Oxygen atom

Molecule of ammonia (NH_3)

- Nitrogen atom

Three hydrogen atoms

MODELS OF MOLECULES

When studying molecules, scientists often use models to represent them. There are two main types: ball-and-spoke models and space-filling models.

In **ball-and-spoke models**, the bonds that hold the atoms together are shown as sticks.

Molecule of water (H_2O)
- Oxygen atom
- Hydrogen atom

Molecule of methane (CH_4)
- Carbon atom
- Hydrogen atom

In **space-filling models**, atoms are shown clinging together.

Molecule of water (H_2O)
- Oxygen atom
- Hydrogen atom

Molecule of methane (CH_4)
- Carbon atom
- Hydrogen atom

Neither model looks like an actual molecule, but they are simple ways of showing the atoms that form the molecule.

Internet links

Go to www.usborne-quicklinks.com for links to the following websites:

Website 1 Learn about molecules with an online activity.

Website 2 Learn about unusual "mirror molecules".

Website 3 An interactive online lesson about molecules.

WATER MOLECULE

A water molecule consists of two different elements: hydrogen and oxygen. The two hydrogen atoms share electrons with the oxygen atom, so each has a complete shell. The oxygen atom uses two electrons (one from each hydrogen atom) to complete its own outer shell. All the atoms become stable.

The oxygen atom contains six electrons in its outer shell. It needs two more electrons to complete its outer shell and become stable.

Each hydrogen atom contains one electron in its shell. They each seek one electron to complete their shells and become stable.

SOLIDS, LIQUIDS AND GASES

Most substances can exist in three different forms: as solids, liquids or gases. These are called the **states of matter**. A solid has a definite volume and shape. A liquid has a definite volume, but its shape changes according to the shape of its container. A gas has neither shape nor volume. It will move to fill the space available.

THE KINETIC THEORY

The theory that explains the properties of solids, liquids and gases is called the **kinetic theory**. It is based on the idea that all substances are made up of moving particles. It explains the properties of solids, liquids and gases in terms of the energy of these particles.

Heating a substance gives the particles more energy, enabling them to move around faster and change from one state to another. (See *Changes of State*, pages 16-17).

Like many scientific theories, the kinetic theory has never been proved. It provides an explanation, though, for how solids, liquids and gases are seen to behave, and why substances change from one state to another.

Movement of particles in solids, liquids and gases

The particles in a solid have the least energy and cannot overcome the attraction between one another. They vibrate, but stay where they are.

Heating a solid gives the particles more energy so they can escape from each other. The solid melts and becomes a liquid.

The particles in a gas have even more energy. They easily move far apart and spread out through the available space.

This is a geyser. Water heated to boiling point under the ground turns from a liquid to a gas (steam) and shoots out of a crack. You can find out more about what causes geysers over the page.

BROWNIAN MOTION

Random movement of particles in a liquid

The movement of particles in liquids and gases is known as **Brownian motion**, named after a British biologist, Robert Brown (1773-1858). In 1827, Brown observed how tiny grains of pollen moved around randomly in a liquid, but he could not explain what caused this movement.

The German-born scientist Albert Einstein (1879-1955) later explained that the movement of particles in a liquid or gas is caused by the particles being hit by the invisible molecules of the fluid in which the particles are floating.

MEASURING SUBSTANCES

Volume is the amount of space occupied by a solid or liquid. It is measured in cubic metres (m³).

You can calculate the volume of a rectangular solid using this formula:

> **Volume =
> Length x Breadth x Height**

The volume of a liquid can be found by pouring the liquid into a measuring cylinder marked with a scale.

Measuring cylinder

The volume of an irregularly shaped solid is measured by finding how much liquid it displaces, using a Eureka can.

Eureka can

1. Eureka can is filled with water to base of spout.

2. Object is put into Eureka can.

3. Volume of displaced water is measured.

The **mass** of a solid, liquid or gas is the amount of matter it contains. This is measured in kilograms. Mass is different from **weight**, which is a measure of the strength of the pull of gravity on an object. Mass is measured by weighing a substance and comparing its mass with a known mass.

Unknown mass   Known mass

Density is the mass of a substance compared with its volume. For example, the same volumes of cork and metal have different densities because the mass of the metal is much greater than that of the cork. Density is found by dividing the mass of an object by its volume, and it is measured in kilograms per cubic metre (kg/m³).

> **Density = $\dfrac{\text{Mass}}{\text{Volume}}$**

The density of a liquid is measured using a **hydrometer**. The hydrometer floats near the surface in a dense liquid, as only a small volume of liquid needs to be displaced to equal the weight of the hydrometer.

Scale marked on hydrometer

See for yourself

You can do an experiment to find the volumes of irregularly shaped solids without using a Eureka can.

You will need a measuring jug, a cake mixing bowl and a washing-up bowl.

First, put your mixing bowl inside the washing-up bowl. Then carefully fill the mixing bowl with water up to the brim.

Now take the object that you want to measure and hold it just on top of the water's surface. Let the object sink into the water. Water will slop over the side of the mixing bowl and be caught in the washing-up bowl.

Object to be measured

Mixing bowl

Washing-up bowl

Take the mixing bowl out of the washing-up bowl. Now pour the water from the washing-up bowl into the measuring jug. The volume of water is equal to the volume of the object.

Internet links

Go to **www.usborne-quicklinks.com** for links to the following websites:

Website 1 An animated introduction to the states of matter.

Website 2 Test yourself with interactive questions on solids, liquids and gases.

Website 3 An explanation of particle behaviour in a solid, a liquid and a gas.

Website 4 Make slimy substances that can't decide if they're solid or liquid.

Website 5 An interactive online lesson about the states of matter.

Website 6 Learn more about the properties of gases.

CHANGES OF STATE

A substance changes from one **state of matter**, that is solid, liquid or gas, to another, depending on its temperature and pressure. When something changes state, heat is produced or lost as the energy of its particles is increased or decreased. Different substances change state at different temperatures.

An ice cream melts and becomes a liquid in the heat of the Sun.

The heat from a flame melts candle wax, but the wax sets as it drips away from the flame and cools.

MELTING AND BOILING

When a solid is heated, its temperature rises and its particles gain energy until it reaches its **melting point**. The particles now have enough energy to break away from their neighbours so the solid melts.

Further heat causes the temperature of the liquid to rise until it reaches its **boiling point** and the particles break free of each other completely. The liquid becomes a gas.

Some substances, for example carbon dioxide, change from gas to solid, or solid to gas, without passing through a liquid form. This is called **sublimation**.

The temperature at which a substance melts or boils changes if it contains traces of any other substances. For instance, ice (the solid form of water) melts at 0°C. Adding salt to the ice lowers its melting point.

This ice melts at a lower temperature than pure water ice because orange juice has been added to it.

When steam cools down, it turns back into water.

GEYSERS

Geysers are jets of boiling hot water and steam that shoot out from the Earth's crust.

They occur when water under the ground is heated by hot rocks and begins to boil.

As the water turns to steam, the pressure builds up in the channels between the rocks. The geyser then erupts, shooting a jet of steam and water high up into the air.

How geysers occur

Water flows into cavities between the rocks under the ground.

Pressure builds as the water heats and expands. Eventually, it turns to steam.

The pressure builds until boiling water and steam shoot out of a crack in the ground.

CONDENSATION

When a gas cools down enough, it **condenses**, becoming a liquid. This is because as it cools down, its particles lose energy and are unable to stay as far away from each other.

Condensation

Water vapour in the air in a room condenses on a cold window. Droplets of water are formed on the inside of the window.

Outdoors

Cold air

Indoors

Warm air

Condensation forms

FREEZING

When a liquid cools enough, it sets or **freezes**, becoming a solid. Its particles lose further energy and are unable to overcome the attraction between each other.

When tiny droplets of water in the atmosphere freeze, they sometimes join together in beautiful patterns of crystals and form snowflakes like these.

PRESSURE

Air pressure has an effect on the melting or boiling point of a substance. The air naturally presses down on the Earth with a force called **atmospheric pressure**. At sea level, this is described as **one atmosphere**, or **standard pressure**.

At sea level, pure water boils at 100°C.

Higher up, the atmospheric pressure is less. It is easier for the particles in liquids to escape into the air, so their boiling points are lower.

At the top of Mount Everest (8,848m above sea level), where the pressure is less than one atmosphere, pure water boils at 71°C.

WATERLESS PLANET

The surface of Mars is dry. Scientists think that this is because the atmospheric pressure is very low, so any water immediately boils away.

Mars is covered by a dry, reddish dust.

SOLID LIQUID OR GAS?

Whether something is classified as a solid, liquid or gas depends on its state at room temperature (20°C).

Mercury melts at -40°C. It is a liquid at room temperature.

Chlorine boils at -35°C so is a gas at room temperature.

See for yourself

Fill a metal container with ice cubes. Stand it in a warm place and leave it for a few minutes. Then look at the container. You will see drops of water on the outside of it.

Water molecules in the warm air lose energy and slow down when they are cooled by the ice. They stick to each other, forming water droplets.

Droplets of water on the side of the can

Internet links

Go to **www.usborne-quicklinks.com** for links to the following websites:

Website 1 Learn how ice-rinks are kept frozen.

Website 2 Find detailed information and pictures of snowflakes.

Website 3 Pictures of geysers.

Website 4 Find out why salt makes ice melt.

Website 5 See how various elements change phase (state) at different temperatures.

HOW LIQUIDS BEHAVE

A **liquid** has a definite volume but it flows and changes shape to fill its container. The particles in a liquid are fairly close together, but have more energy than the particles in a solid, so are free to move about (see *The Kinetic Theory*, page 14).

EVAPORATION

Some of the molecules on the surface of a liquid have more energy than others, and they escape, or **evaporate**, into the air. Liquids are evaporating all the time, even when they are not being heated.

The particles in water (like all liquids) are free to move about.

These particles have enough energy to escape, or evaporate, from the surface of the liquid to form a vapour.

RATE OF EVAPORATION

The **rate of evaporation** increases with any one or a combination of the following:

• an increase in temperature.

• a decrease in pressure. For instance, water evaporates more quickly at the top of Mount Everest, where the atmospheric pressure is less, than it does at sea level.

• the immediate removal of the vapour from above the liquid by a flow of air. This is why washing hung out to dry on a windy day dries more quickly than on a still day.

• an increase in surface area. For instance, a spilled drink will evaporate or dry up more quickly than the same drink in a glass.

COOLING DOWN

When a liquid is evaporating, its temperature falls because the average energy of the molecules that are left in the liquid has fallen.

SURFACE TENSION

The molecules in a liquid are attracted by all the other liquid molecules around them. The ones on the surface, though, are not pulled upwards because there are no liquid molecules above them. They are more attracted to the other liquid molecules than to the air.

This sideways and downwards attraction at the surface creates a force called **surface tension**. It makes a liquid seem to have a "skin".

Molecules at the surface are attracted to each other, and to those below them. This creates surface tension.

Water forms into droplets because surface tension pulls inwards from all sides, keeping the molecules together.

The drips on these leaves form because surface tension pulls molecules of rainwater together.

STRETCHY SKIN

As a result of surface tension, a liquid's surface is like a stretchy skin, strong enough to support very light objects, such as dust or even insects.

Pond skaters can walk on the surface of water as they are not heavy enough to break the skin-like surface tension.

COHESION

Cohesion happens when molecules of one substance are more attracted to each other than to a substance they are touching. Surface tension is an example of this. Molecules at the water's surface try to stay together rather than move towards the air above.

ADHESION

When molecules of a liquid are more attracted to a substance they are touching than to each other, **adhesion** occurs. The liquid adheres (sticks) to the other substance. Water does this when it touches the sides of a glass.

See for yourself

To see how surface tension can support certain objects, try this quick activity.

Fill a container with water. Put a needle on a small piece of tissue paper and lay it gently on the water.

The tissue soon becomes waterlogged and sinks, but the needle stays afloat, supported by surface tension.

Look closely and you will see that the needle actually dents the water's surface.

Internet links

Go to **www.usborne-quicklinks.com** for links to the following websites:

Website 1 Find out how to create giant bubbles.

Website 2 Investigate the power of soap, and do some experiments with surface tension.

Website 3 Discover if hot and cold liquids mix.

Website 4 Easy-to-read information about liquids.

HOW GASES BEHAVE

A **gas** is a substance that has no definite volume or shape. Its particles have enough energy to spread far apart from each other and fill the space available.

Smells, such as the scent of flowers, are gases that travel through the air by diffusion.

DIFFUSION

The molecules in a gas have enough energy to break free of the forces between them (see *The Kinetic Theory*, page 14). They spread out to fill the available space. This is called **diffusion**.

During diffusion, molecules move from an area where they are in higher concentration to one where their concentration is lower. Diffusion stops when the molecules are evenly distributed.

Molecules of a light gas

Molecules of a heavy gas

Molecules of these two gases diffuse together over time. Light gases diffuse faster than heavy ones. ★

This scientist is taking samples of gases emerging from holes in the side of a volcano. Some of the gases are harmful, so the scientist has to wear a breathing mask.

The set-up below shows how two gases mix by diffusion. A jar of air is turned upside down on top of a jar of bromine, which is heavier than air.

After fifteen minutes, the air and bromine in the jars become mixed by diffusion as their molecules spread through the two jars.

Air

Bromine gas

Gases mixed by diffusion ★

PRESSURE, TEMPERATURE AND VOLUME

Gases exert a push on things that they are contained in. This push, called **pressure**, is felt in all directions. It is the rate at which molecules in a gas hit the sides of its container.

Any change in pressure, temperature, or the container's volume will cause a change in the molecules' behaviour.

If the volume of a gas at a constant temperature is decreased, for example by reducing the size of its container, the pressure of the gas increases. This is because the gas molecules hit the walls of the container more frequently.

When heated, the molecules in a gas gain energy, move around faster and become even further apart – the gas expands and becomes less dense. This is why hot-air balloons float – the air inside them is less dense than the air around them.

If a gas is heated but is not allowed to expand, then its pressure increases. This is because the molecules in the gas gain energy, move around more quickly and hit the walls of the container more frequently.

Under the ground, volcanic gases become extremely hot. The pressure builds and builds until they shoot out of cracks and holes in the ground.

Thermometer, to measure temperature.

Pressure of lid and air

Pressure of gas

Gas at constant temperature, pressure and volume

Temperature is the same as before.

Pressure increased to reduce size of container.

Volume decreases, pressure increases.

Temperature increased.

Pressure kept the same as before.

Volume increases until pressures are equal.

Temperature increased.

Pressure increased, to keep volume same as before.

Pressure increases.

★

Balloons stretch as air spreads out to fill them.

See for yourself

Next time you use a balloon pump, see how it uses pressure to fill the balloon with air.

1. When you pump the handle, the volume of the pump's chamber is decreased so the air pressure inside it is increased.

Chamber

2. Air shoots out of the nozzle, into the balloon.

3. A valve in the pump prevents air from being sucked back out of the balloon.

4. Pressure inside the balloon increases so it stretches and expands. Its volume increases.

Internet links

Go to **www.usborne-quicklinks.com** for links to the following websites:

Website 1 Visit a site where you can investigate the properties of bubbles.

Website 2 Watch animations that help explain gas pressure and diffusion.

Website 3 Facts, experiments and online activities about air pressure.

Website 4 Find some experiments with gases to try at home.

Website 5 Discover how gas is involved in making a refrigerator work.

THE ELEMENTS

An **element** is a substance that contains only one kind of atom – the tiny particles of which all substances are made. For example, sulphur, helium and iron are elements: they contain only sulphur, helium or iron atoms and they cannot be broken down into simpler substances.

GROUPING ELEMENTS

So far, 115 elements have been discovered, but only 90 occur naturally on Earth. Elements can be sorted into metals, non-metals and semi-metals and arranged in a table, called the periodic table, which is shown on pages 26-27.

Sulphur molecules

Sulphur is one of the 90 elements that occur naturally on Earth. It is a non-metal. Its molecules, as shown in this diagram, form irregular ring shapes consisting of eight sulphur atoms.

Sulphur atom

METAL ELEMENTS

Over three-quarters of all the elements are **metals**. Most of the metal elements are dense and shiny. They have many uses as they are strong, but can be easily shaped. They are also good conductors of heat and electricity. Metals are usually found combined with other elements in the Earth's crust (see pages 24-25).

These chocolate eggs are wrapped in thin aluminium foil to keep them fresh. Aluminium is the most common metal on Earth.

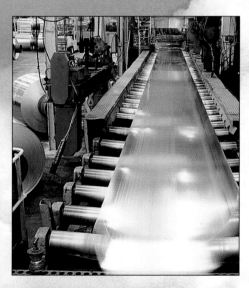

Here, aluminium is rolled into a long, thin sheet. It can be re-shaped easily without breaking because its atoms, which are closely packed, slide over each other.

The Space Shuttle relies on burning elements to blast it into space. It burns the non-metal hydrogen (stored in the red-brown coloured external fuel tank) and powdered aluminium metal (stored in the two white rockets).

USA

United States

NASA Challenger

NON-METALS

There are 16 naturally occurring **non-metal** elements. All (apart from graphite, a form of carbon) are insulators – poor conductors of heat and electricity.

At room temperature, four non-metals (phosphorus, carbon, sulphur and iodine) are solids, and bromine is a liquid. The other 11 non-metals are gases.

Non-metals

Hydrogen	Sulphur
Helium	Chlorine
Carbon	Argon
Nitrogen	Bromine
Oxygen	Krypton
Fluorine	Iodine
Neon	Xenon
Phosphorus	Radon

SEMI-METALS

Semi-metals, also called **metalloids**, can act as poor conductors, just like non-metals. They can also be made to conduct well, like metals. Because of this, semi-metal elements are called **semiconductors**. There are nine semi-metals (see list, right). They are all solids at room temperature.

Semi-metals

Boron	Antimony
Silicon	Tellurium
Germanium	Polonium
Arsenic	Astatine
Selenium	

The semi-metal germanium is used to make transistors* like this one. They are used in radios.

Silicon is used to make integrated circuits* such as this one. Microscopic pathways in the circuit conduct and block electrical pulses.

See for yourself

Finding out how well a substance conducts heat can help to identify whether it is a metal or a non-metal. Try the experiment below.

You will need several long objects such as a metal spoon, a wooden spoon and a plastic ruler. Put a smear of cold butter near the end of each object.

Place the objects in a mug filled with warm water.

Butter

As the heat travels up the object, it melts the butter. You should find that the butter melts on the metal things first, because metals are better conductors of heat than non-metals. Eventually, the warmth of the rising air melts the butter on all the objects.

Internet links

Go to **www.usborne-quicklinks.com** for links to the following websites:

Website 1 Discover elements with activities and quiz.

Website 2 Fun games to help you learn the elements and their symbols.

Website 3 Illustrated element facts.

Website 4 Animated tutorials and online quizzes about metals and non-metals.

Website 5 Try an online quiz and identify metals, non-metals and metalloids.

Website 6 An online lesson about the elements.

ELEMENTS IN THE EARTH

The outermost layer of the Earth is called the **crust**. Most of it is made of only five elements. It is rare for these elements to occur alone, though some, like gold, do. More often they are found together as combined substances called **compounds**. The pure and combined elements found in the crust are called **minerals**. Minerals that contain metals are called **ores**.

Some minerals, such as this chalcedony, can be polished to make beautiful decorative objects.

COMMON ELEMENTS

Oxygen is the most common element in the Earth's crust. It often occurs combined with silicon, the second most common element, and with aluminium and iron, the commonest metals.

This pie chart shows the proportions, by mass, of the five main elements in the Earth's crust.

- ☐ Oxygen 46.6%
- ■ Silicon 27.7%
- ☐ Aluminium 8.1%
- ■ Iron 5%
- ☐ Calcium 3.6%
- ☐ Others 9%

MINERAL FORMATION

Most minerals are formed when hot **magma** (molten rock that contains dissolved gases) pushes up from deep below the Earth's crust, cools and solidifies.

The conditions in the place where magma cools determine which type of mineral forms. Geometric shapes called **crystals** form when minerals cool slowly. The cooling process can be so quick, though, that the mineral has no time to crystallize. A kind of shiny black glass, called obsidian, forms in these conditions.

This picture shows huge clumps of shiny black obsidian jutting out of its surrounding rock.

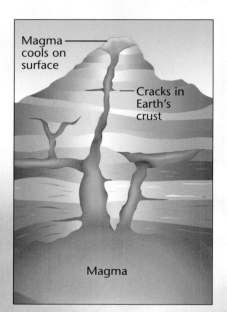

Magma cools on surface

Cracks in Earth's crust

Magma

Molten magma is less dense than the surrounding crust. It rises up through cracks and cools to form minerals.

MINERAL GROUPS

Minerals are divided into groups according to the elements which make them up. Minerals made of a single element are called **native elements**.

Pure silver on a piece of rock

This rock contains specks of pure gold.

Diamonds are crystals of pure carbon. Most are found in a rock called kimberlite, which forms under great heat and pressure.

Silicates, which contain **silica** (silicon combined with oxygen), are the largest group, making up 92% of minerals in the crust.

Beryl is a silicate made up of the elements silicon, oxygen, aluminium and beryllium.

Carbonates are minerals that contain elements combined with carbon and oxygen. They are the most abundant minerals after the silicates.

Smithsonite is zinc carbonate.

Malachite is copper carbonate. It is often polished and used in jewellery.

Halides are a group of minerals which contain halogen* elements.

Rock salt (halite) is formed when salt water evaporates.

Sulphides are a group of minerals that contain elements combined with sulphur.

Sphalerite is made of zinc and sulphur. Most of the world's zinc is mined from this mineral.

Phosphates are minerals formed when phosphorus reacts with oxygen and other elements.

Turquoise is a semi-precious mineral which is a phosphate of aluminium and copper.

Many elements combine with oxygen in the crust to form the group of minerals called **oxides**.

Haematite is a red iron oxide used to produce iron. It is also called "kidney-stone" because of its shape.

There are a number of other mineral groups containing oxygen. These all have names ending in "ate". The first part of their names (see below) show the other elements involved.

Mineral group	Element
Arsenates	Arsenic
Borates	Boron
Chromates	Chromium
Molybdates	Molybdenum
Nitrates	Nitrogen
Sulphates	Sulphur
Tungstates	Tungsten
Vanadates	Vanadium

See for yourself

Rocks are made up of a mixture of minerals. If you look at a rock with a magnifying glass, you can sometimes see the different minerals in it.

Magnified piece of granite

Potassium feldspar

Quartz

Biotite mica

Plagioclase feldspar

Internet links

Go to **www.usborne-quicklinks.com** for links to the following websites:

Website 1 A definition of the term "mineral".

Website 2 Browse an A–Z guide to the Earth's minerals.

Website 3 Find out how to identify minerals, or grow your own crystals.

Website 4 Look at pictures of a collection of minerals.

Website 5 Lots of information on rocks and minerals, with questions to test your knowledge.

* Halogens, 46

THE PERIODIC TABLE

The **periodic table** is an arrangement of the elements placed in order of increasing atomic number (the number of protons in the nucleus). Each element is represented by a box containing its chemical symbol, atomic number and relative atomic mass (see far right). Some versions, such as the one shown here, also give the elements' names. New elements are added when they are discovered.

Structure of an atom

Electron
Proton
Neutron

Nucleus
Shell

READING THE TABLE

The table is arranged into rows and columns. Looking at the table you will see that it has numbered rows (called **periods**) and columns (**groups**).

PERIODS

Each period is numbered, from 1–7. The atoms of all the elements in one period have the same number of shells, which contain electrons. For example, elements in period 2 have two shells and those in period 3 have three.

Moving from left to right across a period, each successive element has one more electron in the outer shell of its atoms. This leads to a fairly regular pattern of change in the chemical behaviour of the elements across a period.

GROUPS

Each group has a Roman numeral, from I-VIII. Elements in the same group have the same number of electrons in their outer shell. This means that, chemically, they behave in similar ways.

Period number — 1

1
H
Hydrogen
1.0

Hydrogen is the lightest element. It has an atomic number of 1. It is not a metal so it is placed separately.

Group number

Key

Each element has a separate box in the periodic table containing the information below.

50
Sn
Tin
118.7

50 — Atomic number
Sn — Chemical symbol
Tin — Name
118.7 — Relative atomic mass

	I	II							
2	3 **Li** Lithium 6.9	4 **Be** Beryllium 9.0							
3	11 **Na** Sodium 23.0	12 **Mg** Magnesium 24.3							
4	19 **K** Potassium 39.1	20 **Ca** Calcium 40.1	21 **Sc** Scandium 45.0	22 **Ti** Titanium 47.9	23 **V** Vanadium 50.9	24 **Cr** Chromium 52.0	25 **Mn** Manganese 54.9	26 **Fe** Iron 55.9	27 **Co** Cobalt 58.9
5	37 **Rb** Rubidium 85.5	38 **Sr** Strontium 87.6	39 **Y** Yttrium 88.9	40 **Zr** Zirconium 91.2	41 **Nb** Niobium 92.9	42 **Mo** Molybdenum 95.9	43 **Tc** Technetium (98)	44 **Ru** Ruthenium 101.1	45 **Rh** Rhodium 102.9
6	55 **Cs** Caesium 132.9	56 **Ba** Barium 137.3	71 **Lu** Lutetium 175.0	72 **Hf** Hafnium 178.5	73 **Ta** Tantalum 181.0	74 **W** Tungsten 183.8	75 **Re** Rhenium 186.2	76 **Os** Osmium 190.2	77 **Ir** Iridium 192.2
7	87 **Fr** Francium (223)	88 **Ra** Radium (226)	103 **Lr** Lawrencium (262)	104 **Rf** Rutherfordium (261)	105 **Db** Dubnium (262)	106 **Sg** Seaborgium (266)	107 **Bh** Bohrium (264)	108 **Hs** Hassium (269)	109 **Mt** Meitnerium (268)

The relative atomic masses for unstable, radioactive* elements are shown in brackets.

The elements with atomic numbers 57-70 belong to period 6.

The elements with atomic numbers 89-102 belong to period 7.

57 **La** Lanthanum 138.9	58 **Ce** Cerium 140.1	59 **Pr** Praseodymium 140.9	60 **Nd** Neodymium 144.2	61 **Pm** Promethium (145)	62 **Sm** Samarium 150.4	63 **Eu** Europium 152.0
89 **Ac** Actinium (227)	90 **Th** Thorium 232.0	91 **Pa** Protactinium 231.0	92 **U** Uranium 238.0	93 **Np** Neptunium (237)	94 **Pu** Plutonium (244)	95 **Am** Americium (243)

* Radioactivity, 60

SIMILAR BEHAVIOUR

On this periodic table, all elements that behave more-or-less in similar ways have the same coloured background. The colour-coding is explained here.

Non-metals
Mostly solid or gas, and non-shiny. Melt and boil at low temperatures.

Semi-metals
Also called metalloids, these have a mixture of the properties of metals and non-metals.

Metals
All are solid (except mercury, a liquid). Generally, they are shiny and have high melting points.

Transition metals are mostly hard and tough. Many are used in industry or jewellery.

Inner-transition metals are rare and tend to react easily with other elements, which makes them difficult to use in their natural state.

RELATIVE ATOMIC MASS

Relative atomic mass is the average mass number of the atoms in a sample of an element. (The mass number is the total number of protons and neutrons in a nucleus.) Moving through the periodic table, elements are progressively heavier. For example, hydrogen (relative atomic mass: 1) is the lightest element. Ruthenium (101.1) is over a hundred times heavier.

GROUPS WITH NAMES

Some of the groups in the periodic table have names. For example, the metals in group I are all alkali metals and group II are alkaline earth metals. The elements in group VII are halogens and group VIII (sometimes called group 0) are called noble gases.

DIFFERENT VERSION

An alternative version of the periodic table shows it split into 18 groups rather than eight. This is achieved by treating each column in the transition metals section of the table as a separate group, numbered from 3-12. In this version, all groups are referred to by ordinary numbers, not Roman numerals.

Transition metals

III	IV	V	VI	VII	VIII
					2 He Helium 4
5 B Boron 10.8	6 C Carbon 12.0	7 N Nitrogen 14.0	8 O Oxygen 16.0	9 F Fluorine 19.0	10 Ne Neon 20.2
13 Al Aluminium 27.0	14 Si Silicon 28.1	15 P Phosphorus 31.0	16 S Sulphur 32.1	17 Cl Chlorine 35.5	18 Ar Argon 39.9

28 Ni Nickel 58.7	29 Cu Copper 63.5	30 Zn Zinc 65.4	31 Ga Gallium 69.7	32 Ge Germanium 72.6	33 As Arsenic 74.9	34 Se Selenium 79.0	35 Br Bromine 79.9	36 Kr Krypton 83.8
46 Pd Palladium 106.4	47 Ag Silver 107.9	48 Cd Cadmium 112.4	49 In Indium 114.8	50 Sn Tin 118.7	51 Sb Antimony 121.8	52 Te Tellurium 127.6	53 I Iodine 126.9	54 Xe Xenon 131.3
78 Pt Platinum 195.1	79 Au Gold 197.0	80 Hg Mercury 200.6	81 Tl Thallium 204.4	82 Pb Lead 207.2	83 Bi Bismuth 209.0	84 Po Polonium (209)	85 At Astatine (210)	86 Rn Radon (222)
110 Dt Darmstadtium (269)	111 Uuu Unununium (272)	112 Uub Ununbium (277)	114 Uuq Ununquadium (285)		116 Uuh Ununhexium (289)			118 Uuo Ununoctium (293)

Inner-transition metals

64 Gd Gadolinium 157.2	65 Tb Terbium 158.9	66 Dy Dysprosium 162.5	67 Ho Holmium 164.9	68 Er Erbium 167.3	69 Tm Thulium 168.9	70 Yb Ytterbium 173.0
96 Cm Curium (247)	97 Bk Berkelium (247)	98 Cf Californium (251)	99 Es Einsteinium (252)	100 Fm Fermium (257)	101 Md Mendelevium (258)	102 No Nobelium (259)

Elements 57-70 are called the **lanthanides** or **rare earths**.

Elements 89-102 are called the **actinides** or **radioactive rare earths**.

METALS

All the metal elements share certain properties. For example, they are shiny and they conduct electricity. They are classified according to the way they behave. For instance some, such as potassium and sodium, are very reactive and react violently with water and air, while others, such as gold, do not react at all.

The centre of the Earth is believed to be made of the metals iron and nickel.

Solid iron and nickel

Molten iron and nickel

Fireworks contain metal compounds that burn with brilliant colours.

PROPERTIES OF METALS

All metals, except for mercury, are solid at room temperature (20°C) and they are good conductors of electricity and heat. They are shiny when cut, and some, such as iron and nickel, are magnetic.

Metals that can be pulled out to make wire are described as **ductile**. Those that can be beaten flat are described as **malleable**.

Flat panel of malleable metal

Metal wire

THE REACTIVITY SERIES

The **reactivity series** is a list of metals showing how reactive they are. The position of each metal is decided by observing how they behave during reactions involving other metals. For instance, more reactive metals pull oxygen from less reactive metals.

Reactive metals are difficult to separate from the minerals in which they are found, while the least reactive metals can be found as pure metals.

Sodium and potassium are stored in oil as they react violently with air and water.

Copper is the least reactive metal that can be produced at a reasonable cost. It is used for pipes, hot-water tanks and electrical wiring.

Reactivity series
Most reactive
Potassium
Sodium
Calcium
Magnesium
Aluminium
Zinc
Iron
Tin
Lead
Copper
Silver
Gold
Platinum
Least reactive

FLAME TESTS

When some metals burn, they produce distinctive coloured flames. Burning a substance can be used as a way to test for the presence of a particular metal. The substance is held in a flame on a piece of unreactive platinum wire.

Potassium during the flame test

Sodium	Copper	Calcium	Barium	Potassium
★				

| Yellow flame | Blue-green flame | Red flame | Green flame | Lilac flame |

IRON AND STEEL

Nearly all iron mined from the Earth is found as an **ore** (that is, combined with another substance). Most of it is made into steel, which is used to make many useful things, ranging from paper clips and tools to frames for giant buildings.

ELEMENT OR ALLOY?

Iron is an element which is extracted mostly from an ore called haematite, a compound of iron and oxygen. **Steel** is an alloy (that is, a mixture) of iron, carbon and traces of other metals.

Magnetite

Haematite

Magnetite and haematite are the two most common iron ores.

MAKING IRON

Iron is extracted from iron ore in a **blast furnace**. In the furnace, iron ore, limestone and **coke** (coal heated to burn off oils and leave carbon) are blasted with very hot air. This process is called **smelting**. The carbon combines with oxygen to form carbon monoxide. The carbon monoxide then becomes carbon dioxide by pulling the oxygen away from the iron ore. This is an example of a reduction* reaction.

The iron extracted from iron ore contains some left-over carbon (about 4%) from the smelting process, plus other impurities such as sulphur. Called **pig iron**, it is used to make cast iron, or refined further to make steel.

The smelting process

1. Iron ore, coke and limestone are fed into the blast furnace. The limestone reacts with the impurities in the ore to produce waste that is called **slag**.

2. Hot air is blasted into the furnace. It reacts with the carbon to form carbon monoxide. This reaction raises the temperature to about 2,000°C. Then the carbon monoxide reacts with the oxygen in the ore leaving the metal free.

3. Molten iron is tapped off here.

4. Molten slag runs out near the bottom of the furnace. This is used in road making.

The furnace is 30m tall.

The blast furnace is kept alight for years until the lining of the walls starts to disintegrate.

The walls are over 3m thick.

The steel frame of this unfinished building will eventually be covered with concrete panels, to create a huge office block like those in the background.

* Reduction, 60.

MAKING STEEL

Steel is made of iron that has been through a blast furnace, with other elements added to make it stronger. To make steel, molten iron is blasted with oxygen, removing more carbon. The oxygen combines with carbon in the iron to form the gas carbon monoxide, which is collected and used as fuel. At the end, the steel may contain as little as 0.04% carbon, although different grades of steel contain different amounts.

To convert iron to steel, molten iron is poured into a furnace called a **converter**.

A high-pressure jet of almost pure oxygen is blasted into the converter. The oxygen combines with the carbon, forming carbon monoxide.

Steel is also made by melting down scrap steel in an **electric arc furnace**. The metal is melted by a powerful current of electricity.

The type of steel used for tools contains up to 1% carbon. This steel is very rigid but brittle. Chromium and vanadium are added to make the tools strong.

Steel that is used in construction, like the frame shown here, is painted to protect it from rusting before it is covered over by the rest of the building. A rusting frame would be dangerously weak.

Steel paper clips contain about 0.08% carbon. This makes them bendy. Those shown here are plastic coated to make them eye-catching.

Internet links

Go to **www.usborne-quicklinks.com** for links to the following websites:

Website 1 See an animated blast furnace and find out how it works.

Website 2 Detailed information about all aspects of steel.

Website 3 Take an interactive look at steel processing and manufacturing.

Website 4 Learn about the properties of steel and how rail tracks are made.

Website 5 Follow an animated recycling tour and find out what happens to metal cans.

MAIN METALS AND ALLOYS

There are 65 metals that naturally exist on Earth. Of these, just 20 are used, on their own or as part of an alloy, to produce nearly all manufactured, metal-based things. You can find out about those metals here, plus the five most common alloys, and see examples of how some of them are used.

This French horn is made of brass, an alloy.

Aluminium
A very light, silvery-white metal that is resistant to corrosion. It is extracted from its ore, bauxite, by electrolysis*. Aluminium is used in overhead electric cables, aircraft, ships, cars, drinks cans and kitchen foil.

Brass
An alloy of copper and zinc. It is easy to shape and is used for decorative ornaments, musical instruments, screws and tacks.

Bronze
An alloy of copper and tin known since ancient times. It resists corrosion and is easy to shape. Coins made of bronze are used as low-value currency in many countries.

Calcium
A malleable, silvery-white metal found in limestone and chalk. It also occurs in animal bones and teeth. It is used to make cement and high-grade steel.

Chromium
A hard, grey metal used to make stainless steel and for plating other metals to protect them or give them a shiny, reflective finish.

Copper
A malleable, reddish metal used to make electrical wires, hot water tanks and the alloys brass, bronze and cupronickel.

Cupronickel
An alloy made from copper and nickel from which most silver-coloured coins are made.

Gold
A soft, unreactive, bright yellow element that is used for jewellery and in electronics.

Iron
A malleable, grey-white magnetic metal extracted mainly from the ore haematite by smelting in a blast furnace. It is used in building and engineering, and to make the alloy steel.

Lead
A heavy, malleable, poisonous blue-white metal extracted from the mineral galena and used in batteries, roofing and as a shield against radiation from X-rays.

Magnesium
A light, silvery-white metal that burns with a bright white flame. It is used in rescue flares and fireworks and in lightweight alloys.

Mercury
A heavy, silvery-white, poisonous liquid metal used in thermometers, dental amalgam for filling teeth, and in some explosives.

Platinum
A malleable, silvery-white unreactive metal used for making jewellery, in electronics and as a catalyst*.

Plutonium
A radioactive metal produced by bombarding uranium (see opposite) in nuclear reactors and used in nuclear weapons.

Potassium
A light, silvery, highly reactive metal. Potassium compounds are used in chemical fertilizers and to make glass.

Three million aluminium fasteners hold this jet's body together.

* Catalyst, Electrolysis, 58.

Silver

A malleable, grey-white metal that is a very good conductor of heat and electricity. It is used for making jewellery, silverware and photographic film.

Sodium

A very reactive, soft, silvery-white metal that occurs in common salt and is used in street lamps and in the chemical industry.

Solder

An alloy of tin and lead that has a low melting point and is used for joining wires in electronics.

Steel

An alloy of iron and carbon that is one of the most important materials in industry. Stainless steel, an alloy of steel and chromium, resists corrosion and is used in aerospace industries.

This Boeing 747 is built using a high-strength alloy that contains mostly aluminium – a very light metal. The jet engines are made of titanium, which is also light, but can easily withstand the enormous temperatures that are generated in the engines.

Tin

A soft, malleable, silvery-white metal. It is used for tin-plating steel to stop it corroding, and in the alloys bronze, pewter and solder.

Titanium

A strong, white, malleable metal. It is very resistant to corrosion and is used in alloys for spacecraft, aircraft and bicycle frames.

Tungsten

A hard, grey-white metal. It is used for lamp filaments, in electronics, and in steel alloys for making sharp-edged cutting tools.

Uranium

A silvery-white, radioactive metal used as a source of nuclear energy and also in nuclear weapons.

Vanadium

A hard, white, poisonous metal used to increase the strength and hardness of steel alloys. A vanadium compound is used as a catalyst* for making sulphuric acid.

Zinc

A blue-white metal extracted from the mineral zinc blende (sphalerite). It is used as a coating on iron to prevent rusting (called galvanizing). It is also used in certain electric batteries and in alloys such as brass.

Internet links

Go to www.usborne-quicklinks.com for links to the following websites:

Website 1 Find out information about the main metals mined in Australia.

Website 2 Read about how metals are extracted from their ores.

Website 3 Discover fascinating facts about gold.

Website 4 Find detailed information about aluminium.

* Catalyst, Galvanizing, 58

RECYCLING METALS

Mining and extracting metals from ores is an expensive process. Fortunately, though, metals can be used again. The process of making them re-usable is called **recycling**, and it is much cheaper than extracting metals from ores. Recycling is done by melting down used metal, to produce a metal that is almost as good as new. It can be done over and over again.

THE RECYCLING PROCESS

Before a metal can be recycled it needs to be collected and separated from any other types of metal. This ensures that the recycled metal is as pure as possible. It is then melted down and poured into moulds. The metal cools into a solid block, ready to be made into a new, finished product.

WHICH METALS?

The most commonly recycled metals are steel and aluminium. However, other metals, such as copper, tin and lead and even precious metals, including gold, silver and platinum, are recycled too.

STEEL

Most steel for recycling comes from scrapped vehicles, such as cars and ships. Old industrial machinery is a good source too. Factories that use steel save offcuts and return them to steelworks to be melted and re-used.

Some of the things that people throw out from their homes, such as old washing machines, also contain steel. Much of this can be recycled.

Here, red-hot recycled steel is being poured into a mould.

This giant electromagnet* is picking up vast quantities of junk iron and steel. The metal will be dumped in a blast furnace to be melted down.

42 *Electromagnet, 58.

ALUMINIUM

Recycled aluminium accounts for about 30% of all aluminium in use. It takes only 5% as much energy to recycle aluminium as it does to extract it from its ore, **bauxite**.

The biggest source of aluminium for recycling is old drinks cans. In North America, over 64 billion aluminium drinks cans are recycled every year. More than half of the aluminium in a drinks can has been recycled.

Crushed aluminium drinks cans, ready to be melted down.

The materials being picked up by this giant magnet all contain iron.

PRECIOUS METALS

Some industries use precious metals. The photographic industry, for example, uses lots of silver, which it recycles to cut costs and preserve resources. A great deal of recycled gold, silver and platinum comes from old jewellery and other ornaments.

When South America was invaded by Spaniards in the sixteenth century, thousands of golden treasures such as this were stolen, melted down and made into new ornaments.

See for yourself

Most drinks cans have information printed on them stating what they are made of. Take a look the next time you have a can of drink. Most likely, the can will be made of aluminium, and it will also have a symbol on it, signifying that it is recyclable.

Internet links

Go to **www.usborne-quicklinks.com** for links to the following websites:

Website 1 Watch an animated presentation about steel and how it is recycled.

Website 2 Fun games and puzzles and facts about recycling steel cans.

Website 3 Take an interactive tour to find out how aluminium is recycled.

Website 4 Further information about aluminium recycling.

Website 5 How aluminium and steel recycling are related to energy use in the USA.

THE HALOGENS

The **halogens** are a group of five elements. They are fluorine, chlorine, bromine, iodine and astatine. They are all very reactive and poisonous and together form group 7 of the periodic table.

Halogen lamps contain compounds of bromine that make them shine really brightly.

FLUORINE

Fluorine is a poisonous gas. It is extracted from the mineral fluorite. **Fluorides** (non-poisonous compounds of fluorine) are added to toothpaste and drinking water to reduce tooth decay.

Toothpaste and water containing fluoride

Fluorine is also combined with carbon to make useful compounds called **fluorocarbons**. An example is PTFE (polytetrafluoroethene), which is used as a non-stick coating on frying pans and skis.

These skis have a coating of PTFE on their undersides. This non-stick layer helps them to slide freely over snow and ice.

This huge salt flat in South America contains sodium iodate. This is collected and used to produce the halogen iodine.

CHLORINE

On its own, **chlorine** is a poisonous gas. It is very reactive and only occurs naturally in compounds such as sodium chloride (common salt). Chlorine is used as a disinfectant and to make hydrochloric acid and PVC (polyvinylchloride) plastic.

Compounds of chlorine have many uses. **Sodium hypochlorite**, for example, is used to make household bleach, and to bleach paper pulp so that it turns white.

This juggling equipment is made from PVC.

Writing paper is bleached using sodium hypochlorite, a compound of chlorine.

BROMINE

Bromine is a foul-smelling brown liquid. Traces of bromine are found in sea water and mineral springs. Compounds of bromine and one other element are called **bromides**. Silver bromide is used in photographic film.

When light hits silver bromide on photographic film, a reaction takes place in different layers of the film, creating various-coloured patches.

Bromine compounds are used to make rat poisons and products that treat wood for termite infestation.

IODINE

Iodine is a purple-black solid. It is used in medicine, photography and dyes, and is produced in large quantities from sodium iodate.

Traces of iodine are found in foods, and without it the cells in our bodies would not be able to convert food into energy. However, large quantities of iodine are harmful.

Iodine is found in seaweed, and in vegetables and fruit.

ASTATINE

Astatine is an unstable, radioactive element. It is the heaviest of all halogens, but hardly any of it is found in nature. Scientists estimate that only about 30g of astatine exists in the entire Earth's crust. They have been able to create more than 20 different astatine isotopes* during experiments, though.

See for yourself

You can buy iodine solution from a pharmacy and use it to test for the presence of starch. Drip some drops onto slices of food, such as raw potato, apple and a piece of bread. If starch is present, the food will turn blue-black very quickly.

This type of dropper is called a pipette.

Iodine tastes unpleasant, so make sure that you don't get any in your mouth.

Internet links

Go to **www.usborne-quicklinks.com** for links to the following websites:

Website 1 Try out an activity designed to show how fluoride can help to protect teeth from decay.

Website 2 Lots of information about chlorine, including a description of what it is and some of its many uses.

Website 3 Discover the difference between halogen light bulbs and normal light bulbs, and why halogen bulbs are more efficient.

Website 4 Find detailed information about each halogen (F, Cl, Br, I, and At).

* Isotopes, 11.

CARBON

Carbon is a solid non-metallic element found in all living things. It occurs as a **free element** (on its own) mainly in the forms of hard, colourless diamond and crumbly black graphite.

FORMS OF CARBON

Carbon atoms can bond* together in different ways. These different forms are called **allotropes**. They contain the same types of atoms, but are bonded together in different ways. Carbon has three main allotropes – diamond, graphite and buckminsterfullerene.

DIAMOND

In **diamond**, each carbon atom is bonded to four other atoms. This makes diamond very hard – it is the hardest substance found in nature. Diamond forms naturally as tetrahedral (four-sided) crystals.

Carbon atom in diamond

*

The crystal structure of a diamond sparkles brilliantly, and diamonds are valued for their beauty. They can be several different colours. The purest ones are transparent and are used to make jewellery.

Diamonds are cut in such a way that their surfaces split up light into the colours of the rainbow.

The large diamond in this sceptre is the Star of Africa. It is about 6cm long and is the largest cut diamond in the world. The sceptre belongs to the British monarch.

* Bond, 58.

DIAMOND VARIETIES

Impure varieties of diamond, such as **carbonado** (also called **black diamond**) are valued in industry for their hardness. They are used in cutting and drilling equipment, as well as in some very accurate watches.

Naturally occuring varieties of diamonds are mined from the Earth, but diamonds can also be manufactured. These synthetic diamonds are created by mixing graphite with a catalyst* and subjecting it to great heat and pressure.

GRAPHITE

In **graphite** (sometimes called **plumbago**), each atom of carbon is bonded to three other atoms, arranged in a honeycomb-like network of plates that easily slide over each other. This makes graphite soft and flaky. The plate network is held together by weak forces.

Carbon atom
in graphite

The weak forces between the plates give graphite a very slippery structure. This makes graphite a very good lubricant, and it is used to reduce friction between the moving parts of machines. The weak forces also mean it is a good conductor of electricity so it is often used to make electrodes*.

Pencil "leads" are in fact made from powdered graphite mixed with clay. Soft pencils contain more graphite than hard ones.

BUCKMINSTERFULLERENE

Buckminsterfullerene is an allotrope of carbon discovered in 1985. Each molecule contains 60 carbon atoms linked in the shape of a hollow ball. It is formed by heating graphite in helium until it vaporizes, and then letting it cool and condense.

A buckminsterfullerene molecule

Buckminsterfullerene molecules are sometimes called **buckyballs**. Their atoms are arranged in a pattern of hexagons and pentagons similar to that on soccer balls.

Due to their robust spherical structure, buckyballs are really strong – a hundred times stronger than steel, but only a sixth of its weight.

Using a method similar to that for making buckyballs, scientists can also make tiny **nanotubes**. They hope to use them to build super-strong materials.

Nanotubes – made by vaporizing graphite with a laser and adding a metal catalyst*.

See for yourself

Take a look at your pencils, and compare the darkness of the lines that they make. A pencil containing more graphite than clay gives a darker, smudgier line than one that has more clay than graphite.

Letters and numbers printed on the side of a pencil indicate its graphite/clay content. A number followed by a B (for black) means that it has more graphite than clay. A number followed by an H (for hard) means it has more clay than graphite.

A medium pencil, one that gives lines that are neither dark nor light, has HB written on it.

This 4B pencil gives a soft, dark line. 9B is the darkest.

This 2H pencil gives a light, grey line. 9H is the lightest.

Internet links

Go to **www.usborne-quicklinks.com** for links to the following websites:

Website 1 Find out about carbon.

Website 2 Read about extraterrestrial gases found in unusual carbon molecules nicknamed "buckyballs".

Website 3 Lots of information about diamonds.

Website 4 More fascinating facts about diamonds.

Website 5 Find out why carbon can be both hard and soft.

Website 6 Information about buckminsterfullerene.

Catalyst, Electrode, 58.

THE CARBON CYCLE

Most carbon atoms have existed since the world began. They circulate through animals, plants and the air in a process called the **carbon cycle**.

Plants use carbon dioxide to make carbon compounds by photosynthesis*. Animals eat plants (or other animals) and use the carbon compounds in their bodies. Carbon dioxide returns to the air when fuels burn and living things decay, and as a result of internal respiration, which is the way plants and animals break down sugars to release energy.

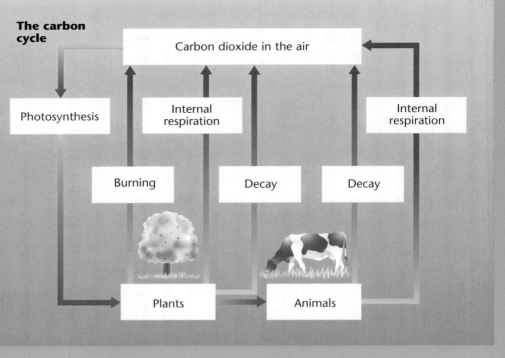

The carbon cycle

Carbon dioxide in the air → Photosynthesis → Internal respiration → Burning → Decay → Decay → Plants → Animals

CARBON COMPOUNDS

Carbon atoms can bond with up to four other atoms, including other carbon atoms. This allows carbon to combine to form a vast number of different compounds. There are many more compounds of carbon than of any other element. All those compounds of carbon that are found in living things are called **organic compounds**.

Like all living things, both this kingfisher and the branch it is sitting on are made from compounds of carbon.

CARBON FIBRES

Silky threads of pure carbon, called **carbon fibres**, are used to reinforce plastics. This material is used to make lightweight boats and tennis racquets. A racing bike made of carbon fibre is eight times stronger than a steel one, but many times lighter.

This bike's frame is made from carbon fibre.

CARBON MIXTURES

Carbon can be found mixed with other elements and compounds. **Coal**, for example, is mainly carbon, but contains hydrogen, oxygen, nitrogen and sulphur. It is a **fossil fuel**, that is, a fuel formed over millions of years from the remains of plants.

There are three types of coal, containing varying amounts of carbon. **Lignite**, also called brown coal, only has 60-70% carbon. **Bituminous coal**, which is shiny and black, has more than 80%. **Anthracite** has more than 90% carbon.

Charcoal is another impure form of carbon. To make it, wood is heated in an airtight space. This removes the chemicals that produce wood smoke, leaving flaky black chunks of charcoal, which burn cleanly when ignited.

Unlike diamond and graphite, neither coal nor charcoal have a regular structure.

USING COAL AND CHARCOAL

Coal is an important fuel. Over a third of the world's electricity is produced by power stations that burn coal. Lignite is cheap and plentiful, but produces a lot of pollution. Bituminous coal and anthracite are better since they cause less air pollution.

Power stations fuelled by coal can produce an average of 600 megawatts of electrical energy in an hour.

Charcoal burns without smoke. This makes it an ideal heat source for barbecues, because it cooks things without coating them in soot.

A form of charcoal called **activated charcoal** is used in filters and gas masks to remove poisonous fumes. It has countless tiny holes in its surface, which are ideal for trapping fumes. It is made by allowing charcoal to burn briefly in oxygen at the end of the charcoal-making process.

Charcoal is often used as a fuel on barbecues, and can be shaped into sticks to be used as an artists' drawing material.

See for yourself

The next time you see coal burning, try to imagine what is happening to the molecules that it is made of.

The heat gives the molecules enough energy to break apart. This gives off heat energy. As the bonds break, atoms, such as hydrogen, are freed from the molecules. These liberated atoms burn too, giving off additional heat.

Internet links

Go to **www.usborne-quicklinks.com** for links to the following websites:

Website 1 Key facts about carbon.

Website 2 An animated presentation and quiz about the carbon cycle.

Website 3 Read some detailed information about the formation of coal.

Website 4 Learn more about coal mining with a virtual tour of a mine shaft.

Website 5 Become a secret agent and carry out interactive chemistry missions.

SULPHUR

The element **sulphur** is a bright yellow, crumbly solid. It is found in underground deposits in volcanic areas. It is also found in minerals such as iron pyrites and copper pyrites.

Pure sulphur

Iron pyrites, a compound of iron and sulphur

FORMS OF SULPHUR

Sulphur molecules form in crooked rings of eight atoms, sometimes referred to as crowns. The rings can combine together in different ways to make two distinct crystal forms, known as allotropes.

Most sulphur is found in the form of **rhombic sulphur**.

Sulphur becomes a gas at 444°C. The molecules split apart and float freely, as shown here.

Rhombic sulphur crystal

The molecules fit together closely in rhombic sulphur.

Above 96°C, **monoclinic sulphur** forms. Monoclinic sulphur crystals are long, thin and angular. They look a little like needles.

Monoclinic sulphur crystal

The molecules are less closely packed than in rhombic sulphur, so it is less dense.

PRODUCING SULPHUR

Most sulphur is obtained from fossil fuels*. It is also extracted from underground deposits by melting it with pressurized steam. This is called the **Frasch process**.

USES OF SULPHUR

One of the most important uses of sulphur is in the manufacture of **sulphuric acid**, which is used to make fertilizers, plastics and batteries. It is also used to **vulcanize** rubber (harden it), in black gunpowder and in medicines.

SULPHUR DIOXIDE

Sulphur burns with a blue flame to form **sulphur dioxide**, a poisonous gas made of sulphur and oxygen. This gas is used to kill insects, as a fungicide and as a preservative for fruit.

Sulphur dioxide can be used to preserve the colour of dried apricots.

Internet links

Go to **www.usborne-quicklinks.com** for links to the following websites:

Website 1 Facts about the discovery, uses and chemistry of sulphur.

Website 2 Find out how sulphur dioxide causes acid rain, and find out where it comes from.

Website 3 Explore a volcano crater and see sulphur crystals and gases that have emerged from vents.

*Fossil fuels, 58.

PHOSPHORUS

Phosphorus is a non-metallic element. It occurs naturally in bones, teeth and the chemicals in the body that store energy. It is also found in the Earth, for example in the mineral apatite. Its most reactive form, white phosphorus, glows in the dark.

The minerals apatite (left) and turquoise (right) contain phosphorus.

FORMS OF PHOSPHORUS

Phosphorus occurs in three crystal forms, or allotropes.

White phosphorus is a poisonous, waxy, white solid that ignites easily when it is exposed to air.

Red phosphorus is a non-poisonous, dark red powder. It is made by heating white phosphorus without air. It is less reactive than white phosphorus.

Black phosphorus is made by heating white phosphorus under pressure using mercury as a catalyst*. Its name comes from its appearance, which is much like graphite. It is the least reactive form of phosphorus.

See for yourself

Take a look at the list of ingredients on a tube of toothpaste.

The list will probably include certain phosphates, such as sodium phosphate and trisodium phosphate. These are compounds that contain phosphorus.

These phosphates are used in toothpastes because they help to loosen stain-forming chemicals from your teeth, helping to keep them white.

USES OF PHOSPHORUS

One of the main uses of phosphorus is in the production of **phosphoric acid** (H_3PO_4). This is used to make iron and steel rust-proof, and also in the manufacture of fizzy drinks.

Phosphoric acid is used to add fizz and flavour to cola drinks.

Red phosphorus is used in matches, pesticides, alloys and distress flares.

White phosphorus is used in rat poison.

When a match is struck, the red phosphorus becomes white phosphorus, burning fiercely in the air.

Compounds of phosphorus and oxygen are called **phosphates**. Phosphates are important in animal and plant growth. They are added to animal feed and used to make fertilizers.

Farm crops, like this cabbage, are fed with large amounts of phosphate-rich fertilizers.

Internet links

Go to **www.usborne-quicklinks.com** for links to the following websites:

Website 1 Essential information about phosphorus.

Website 2 Facts and chemical data about phosphorus.

Website 3 Find out how phosphorus plays an important part in your diet, what it does for different parts of your body, and why too much is bad for you.

* Catalyst, 58

FACTS AND LISTS

PROPERTIES OF ELEMENTS

Here you will find data on the history and physical properties of most of the elements. Recently discovered elements such as ununhexium, about which little is known, are not included. "Year of discovery" is the year in which an element was first isolated. The figures shown are as accurate as possible, but there are different ways of measuring things, so you may find slightly different figures elsewhere.

Element	Melting point (°C)	Boiling point (°C)	Density (g/cm^3)	Discovered by	Year of discovery
Actinium	1,050	3,200	10.1	Debierne	1899
Aluminium	660	2,467	2.7	Oersted	1825
Americium	994	2,607	11.7	Seaborg and others	1944
Antimony	630	1,750	6.62	-	Early historic
Argon	-189	-186	N/A	Rayleigh and Ramsay	1894
Arsenic	-	Sublimes	5.73	Albertus Magnus	1250
Barium	725	1,640	3.51	Davy	1808
Berkelium	986	Unknown	13.3	Seaborg and others	1949
Beryllium	1,278	2,970	1.85	Vauquelin	1798
Bismuth	271	560	9.78	Unknown	15th century
Boron	2,300	2,550	2.34	Gay-Lussac and Thénard; Davy	1808
Bromine	-7.2	59	3.12	Balard	1826
Cadmium	320	765	8.65	Stromeyer	1817
Caesium	28	678	1.9	Bunsen and Kirchoff	1860
Calcium	842	1,484	1.54	Davy	1808
Carbon*	3,730	4,830	3.51	-	Prehistoric
Cerium	798	3,257	6.78	Berzelius and Hisinger	1803
Chlorine	-101	-34	N/A	Scheele	1774
Chromium	1,857	2,672	7.19	Vauquelin	1797
Cobalt	1,495	2,870	8.7	Brandt	1735
Copper	1,083	2,567	8.89	-	Prehistoric
Curium	1,340	3,110	13.51	Seaborg and others	1944
Dysprosium	1,409	2,335	8.56	Boisbaudran	1886
Erbium	1,522	2,510	9.16	Mosander	1843
Europium	822	1,597	5.24	Demarcay	1901
Fluorine	-219	-188	N/A	Moissan	1886
Gadolinium	1,311	3,233	7.95	Marignac	1880
Gallium	29	2,403	5.93	Boisbaudran	1875
Germanium	937	2,830	5.4	Winkler	1886
Gold	1,064	2,807	19.3	-	Prehistoric
Hafnium	2,227	4,602	13.3	Coster and von Hevesy	1923
Helium	-272	-268	N/A	Ramsay	1895
Holmium	1,470	2,720	8.8	Delafontaine and Soret	1878
Hydrogen	-259	-252	N/A	Cavendish	1766
Indium	156	2,080	7.3	Reich and Richter	1863
Iodine	113	184	4.93	Cortois	1811
Iridium	2,410	4,130	22.4	Tennant	1803
Iron	1,535	2,750	7.85	-	Prehistoric
Krypton	-156	-152	N/A	Ramsay and Travers	1898
Lanthanum	920	3,454	6.19	Mosander	1839
Lead	327	1,740	11.3	-	Prehistoric
Lithium	180	1,347	0.53	Arfvedson	1817

* All entries refer to carbon in its graphite form.

Element	Melting point (°C)	Boiling point (°C)	Density (g/cm³)	Discovered by	Year of discovery
Lutetium	1,656	3,315	9.84	Urbain	1907
Magnesium	648	1,090	1.74	Black	1755
Manganese	1,244	1,962	7.2	Gahn, Scheele and Bergman	1774
Mercury	-39	357	13.6	-	Prehistoric
Molybdenum	2,617	4,612	10.1	Scheele	1778
Neodymium	1,010	3,127	7.0	Von Welsbach	1885
Neon	-248	-246	N/A	Ramsay and Travers	1898
Neptunium	640	3,902	20.4	McMillan and Abelson	1940
Nickel	1,453	2,732	8.8	Cronstedt	1751
Niobium	2,468	4,742	8.57	Hatchett	1801
Nitrogen	-209	-196	N/A	Rutherford	1772
Osmium	3,045	5,027	22.5	Tennant	1803
Oxygen	-218	-183	N/A	Priestley	1774
Palladium	1,554	2,963	12.2	Wollaston	1803
Phosphorus	44	280	1.82	Brandt	1669
Platinum	1,772	3,827	21.5	de Ulloa	1735
Plutonium	641	3,232	19.8	Seaborg and others	1940
Polonium	254	962	9.4	Curie	1898
Potassium	63	759	0.86	Davy	1807
Praseodymium	931	3,212	6.78	Von Welsbach	1885
Promethium	1,080	2,460	7.3	Marinsky and others	1945
Radium	700	1,140	5	P. and M. Curie	1898
Radon	-71	-62	N/A	Dorn	1900
Rhenium	3,180	5,627	20.5	Noddack, Berg and Tacke	1925
Rhodium	1,966	3,727	12.4	Wollaston	1803
Rubidium	39	1,270	1.53	Bunsen and Kirchoff	1861
Ruthenium	2,310	3,900	12.3	Sniadecki	1808
Samarium	1,072	1,778	7.54	Boisbaudran	1879
Scandium	1,539	2,832	2.99	Nilson	1879
Selenium	217	685	4.79	Berzelius	1817
Silicon	1,410	2,355	2.35	Berzelius	1824
Silver	961	2,212	10.5	-	Prehistoric
Sodium	98	883	0.97	Davy	1807
Strontium	769	1,384	2.62	Davy	1808
Sulphur	119	444	2.07	-	Prehistoric
Tantalum	2,996	5,425	16.6	Ekeberg	1802
Technetium	2,172	4,877	11.5	Perrier and Segré	1937
Tellurium	449	990	6.2	Von Reichenstein	1782
Terbium	1,360	3,041	8.27	Mosander	1843
Thallium	303	1,457	11.8	Crookes	1861
Thorium	1,750	4,790	11.7	Berzelius	1828
Thulium	1,545	1,950	9.33	Cleve	1879
Tin	232	2,270	7.3	-	Prehistoric
Titanium	1,660	3,287	4.54	Gregor	1791
Tungsten	3,410	5,660	19.3	J. and F. Elhuijar	1783
Uranium	1,132	3,818	19.1	Peligot	1841
Vanadium	1,890	3,380	5.96	del Rio	1801
Xenon	-107	-111	N/A	Ramsay and Travers	1898
Ytterbium	824	1,193	6.98	Marignac	1878
Yttrium	1,523	3,337	4.34	Gadolin	1794
Zinc	419	907	7.1	-	Prehistoric
Zirconium	1,852	3,580	6.49	Klaproth	1789

LAWS

Avogadro's law All gases of the same volume at the same temperature and pressure must contain the same number of molecules.

Bernoulli's principle When the flow of a fluid (for example, air) gets faster, its pressure is reduced.

Boyle's law The pressure and volume of a gas at a constant temperature are inversely proportional.

Charles' law (or **law of volumes**) The volume of an ideal gas at a constant temperature is proportional to its kelvin temperature.

FAMOUS SCIENTISTS

Here are details of some of the scientists who have advanced our understanding of matter and the elements.

Avogadro, Amedeo (1776-1856) This Italian chemist devised Avogadro's law (see above).

Becquerel, Antoine (1852-1908) A French physicist who discovered radioactivity in 1896.

Bohr, Niels (1885-1962) A Danish physicist who applied the quantum theory of physics (see page 60) to Rutherford's structure of the atom in 1913.

Boyle, Robert (1627-1691) This Irish scientist proposed that matter is made up of tiny particles. He also formulated Boyle's law (see above).

Brown, Robert (1773-1858) A Scottish biologist who noted the apparently random motion of particles suspended in liquids. This is called Brownian motion.

Cavendish, Henry (1731-1810) This English chemist and physicist discovered hydrogen, the chemical make-up of air and water, and estimated the weight of the Earth.

Chadwick, James (1891-1974) An English physicist who worked on radioactivity and discovered the neutron.

Charles, Jacques (1746-1823) A French physicist who formulated Charles' law (see above).

Curie, Marie (1867-1934) A pioneering Polish scientist who carried out work on radiation and discovered the radioactive material radium in 1898.

Dalton, John (1766-1844) This English chemist suggested that elements are made of atoms which combine to form compounds.

Lavoisier, Antoine (1743-1794) This French lawyer and scientist named oxygen and hydrogen, and explained the role of oxygen in combustion.

Mendeleyev, Dmitri (1834-1907) This Russian chemist devised the periodic table of elements.

Rutherford, Ernest (1871-1937) A New Zealand-born physicist who demonstrated the structure of the atom.

MOHS HARDNESS SCALE

The hardness of minerals is measured on the **Mohs scale**, named after the German mineralogist, Friedrich Mohs (1773-1839). The scale has a sample mineral for each value, ranging from 1 – soft, crumbly talc, to 10 – diamond.

1. Talc
Very easily scratched with a fingernail.

2. Gypsum
Can be scratched with a fingernail.

3. Calcite
Very easily scratched with a knife, and just with a copper coin.

4. Fluorite
Easily scratched with a knife.

5. Apatite
Just scratched with a knife.

6. Orthoclase
Cannot be scratched with a knife. Just scratches glass.

7. Quartz
Scratches glass easily.

8. Beryl or topaz
Scratches glass very easily.

9. Corundum
Cuts glass.

10. Diamond
Cuts glass very easily. Will scratch corundum.

TEST YOURSELF

1. Electrons are present
A. only in liquid or solid matter
B. only in electrical conductors
C. in all forms of matter   *(Page 8)*

2. An atom usually has equal numbers of
A. neutrons and electrons
B. electrons and protons
C. protons and neutrons   *(Page 9)*

3. The mass number of an atom of an element is the number of
A. protons and neutrons
B. protons
C. electrons   *(Page 10)*

4. Atoms which have the same number of protons and electrons but a different number of neutrons are
A. isomers
B. isotopes
C. allotropes   *(Page 11)*

5. The chemical symbol of iron is
A. F
B. I
C. Fe   *(Page 13)*

6. The chemical symbol of gold is
A. Go
B. Au
C. Ag   *(Page 13)*

7. The kinetic theory explains
A. energy changes
B. moving objects
C. the properties of solids, liquids and gases   *(Page 14)*

8. Sublimation occurs when
A. solids change to gas
B. solids change to liquid
C. liquids change to gas   *(Page 16)*

9. Condensation is when
A. gas changes to liquid
B. gas changes to solid
C. liquid changes to gas   *(Page 17)*

10. A substance is classified as a solid, liquid or gas depending on
A. its state at 0°C
B. its state at 20°C
C. its state at 100°C   *(Page 17)*

11. Gases have
A. definite volume and shape
B. no definite volume and shape
C. definite volume but can change shape   *(Page 20)*

12. How many elements are there?
A. about 20
B. about 50
C. about 100   *(Page 22)*

13. Almost all non-metals are
A. liquids at room temperature
B. poor insulators
C. poor conductors   *(Page 23)*

14. The most common element in the Earth's crust is
A. aluminium
B. oxygen
C. silicon   *(Page 24)*

15. The periodic table is organized into periods of elements which are
A. arranged in columns
B. arranged in rows
C. arranged in clusters   *(Page 26)*

16. The lightest element, with an atomic number of 1, is
A. hydrogen
B. nitrogen
C. oxygen   *(Page 26)*

17. Metals are ductile, which means they can be
A. beaten flat into sheets
B. pulled out to make a wire
C. polished   *(Page 28)*

18. In a flame test, potassium gives
A. a red flame
B. an orange flame
C. a lilac flame   *(Page 29)*

19. In water, alkali metals form
A. acidic solutions
B. alkaline solutions
C. neutral solutions   *(Page 30)*

20. Noble metals are
A. always found in compounds
B. extremely reactive
C. very unreactive   *(Page 30)*

21. Brass is a mixture of
A. copper and zinc
B. copper and tin
C. copper and nickel   *(Page 33)*

22. Bronze is a mixture of
A. copper and zinc
B. copper and tin
C. copper and gold   *(Page 33)*

23. Which gas is needed for corrosion to take place?
A. sulphur dioxide
B. carbon dioxide
C. oxygen   *(Page 38)*

24. One of the oldest known metals is
A. aluminium
B. gold
C. zinc   *(Page 40)*

25. The most abundant element in the universe is
A. aluminium
B. hydrogen
C. oxygen   *(Page 44)*

26. Which element is not a halogen?
A. chlorine
B. iodine
C. phosphorus   *(Pages 46-47, 53)*

27. Elements which exist in differently bonded forms are
A. alloys
B. allotropes
C. isotopes   *(Page 48)*

28. Which of the following substances is not a form of carbon?
A. diamond
B. sulphur
C. graphite   *(Pages 48-49, 52)*

29. One of the main uses of sulphur is
A. making sulphur dioxide
B. in food preservation
C. making sulphuric acid   *(Page 52)*

30. Which of the following is not a form of phosphorus?
A. yellow
B. red
C. white   *(Page 53)*

Answers
1.C 2.B 3.A 4.B 5.C 6.B 7.C 8.A 9.A 10.B 11.B 12.C 13.C 14.B 15.B 16.A 17.B 18.C 19.B 20.C 21.A 22.B 23.C 24.B 25.B 26.C 27.B 28.B 29.C 30.A

57

A-Z OF SCIENTIFIC TERMS

Acid A compound that contains hydrogen and dissolves in water to produce hydrogen ions.

actinides (also **radioactive rare earths** or **radioactive rare-earth metals**) A sub-group of the inner transition metals that includes actinium. All members of the sub-group have radioactive properties.

activated charcoal A form of charcoal (impure carbon) used to remove poisonous fumes, used, for example, in gas masks.

adhesion The attraction of the molecules of one substance to the molecules of another substance they are touching, rather than to each other (see also *cohesion*).

alkali Any **base** (the chemical opposite of an acid) that can dissolve in water, making an alkaline solution.

alkali metals The six very reactive metals that form group I of the periodic table. They are lithium, sodium, potassium, rubidium, caesium and francium.

alkaline earth metals The six metals that form group II of the periodic table. They are beryllium, magnesium, calcium, strontium, barium and radium.

allotropes Different forms in which certain elements, such as carbon, can exist. In each allotrope the same atoms are bonded together in a different way.

alloy A mixture of two or more metals, or a metal and a non-metal.

anodizing A method of coating a metal with a thin layer of its oxide using electrolysis, in order to prevent corrosion.

anthracite The purest form of coal, containing over 90% carbon.

atmosphere 1. The protective layer of air around the Earth that enables plants and animals to live. 2. The unit of atmospheric pressure at sea level.

atmospheric pressure The force of the air pressing down on the Earth's surface. At sea level, atmospheric pressure is one atmosphere (1 atm), also known as **standard pressure** and equivalent to 101,325 pascals.

atomic number The number of protons in the nucleus of an atom.

atoms The tiny particles from which elements are made. Each atom has a positively charged nucleus, consisting of protons and (except hydrogen) neutrons. This is usually balanced by enough negatively charged electrons to make the atom electrically neutral. See also *ion*; *isotopes*.

Ball-and-spoke model A way of representing molecules showing atoms as balls and the chemical bonds joining them as sticks.

bauxite The natural form of aluminium oxide. It is the ore from which aluminium is extracted.

black diamond See *carbonado*.

black phosphorus The least reactive allotrope of phosphorus, made by heating white phosphorus under pressure.

blast furnace A furnace used to smelt iron ore.

boiling point The temperature at which a substance turns from a liquid into a gas.

bond A force that holds together two or more atoms. Atoms make bonds in different ways, depending on their structure.

brown coal See *lignite*.

Brownian motion The movement of microscopic particles, such as dust, in liquids and gases, caused by constant collisions with rapidly moving molecules.

buckminsterfullerene A very strong allotrope of carbon with spherical molecules (often called buckyballs) containing 60 atoms.

Carbohydrates Organic compounds containing carbon, hydrogen and oxygen. They are broken down by all living things to give energy for life.

carbon An element found in compounds in all living things and also occurring naturally as diamond and graphite.

carbonado (or **black diamond**) An impure form of diamond used for cutting in industry because of its hardness.

carbon cycle The process by which carbon (as carbon dioxide) enters the food chain from the atmosphere through photosynthesis and returns to the atmosphere through respiration and decay. See also *internal respiration*.

carbon dioxide (CO_2) A gas with one carbon atom and two oxygen atoms in each molecule.

carbon fibres Silky threads of pure carbon, used to reinforce plastics.

catalyst A substance that changes the rate of a chemical reaction but is itself left unchanged.

catalytic converter A device fitted to cars which uses metal catalysts, for example platinum and rhodium, to remove toxic gases from the exhaust fumes.

CFCs (**chlorofluorocarbons**) Organic compounds of carbon, fluorine and chlorine, that are believed to damage the atmosphere.

chemical formula A combination of chemical symbols, showing the atoms of which a substance is made and their proportions.

chemical reaction An interaction between substances in which their atoms are rearranged to form new substances.

chemical symbol A shorthand way of representing a specific element in formulae and equations.

chlorofluorocarbons See *CFCs*.

cohesion The attraction of the molecules of a substance to each other, rather than to the molecules of a substance they are touching (see also *adhesion*).

combustion The scientific term for all forms of burning.

composites Synthetic materials, especially plastics, made up of different substances combined to improve their properties.

compound A substance made up of two or more elements whose atoms are chemically bonded.

condensation 1. The process of a gas cooling to form a liquid. 2. The droplets of liquid that form as a gas cools.

conductor A substance through which an electric current can flow, or through which heat can flow easily.

corrosion The process by which the surface of a metal reacts with oxygen to form the oxide of the metal, which then either protects the surface, or flakes off to cause damage. See also *rust*.

crust The outermost rock layer of the Earth. Below it is a layer called the **mantle**.

crystal A substance which has solidified in a definite geometrical form, with straight edges and flat surfaces.

Density A measure of the mass of a substance compared with its volume. See also *relative density*.

dental amalgam An alloy of mercury and copper used for filling tooth cavities.

diamond An allotrope of carbon with each atom linked to four others in a tight formation, forming extremely hard, four-sided crystals.

diffusion The spreading out of a gas to fill the space available.

ductile The term that describes a metal which can be stretched out to make wire.

Elastic The term describing something that can be stretched out of shape or size by a force, but returns to its original form when the force is removed (unless it exceeds its elastic limit). See also *plastic*.

elastic limit The point beyond which an elastic substance is altered and weakened permanently by stretching.

electric charge A property of matter which causes electric forces between particles. Opposite charges attract, while like charges repel each other.

electricity The effect caused by the presence or movement of electrically charged particles.

electrode In electrolysis, a conductor through which the current enters or leaves the solution.

electrolysis A method of splitting the elements in a compound by passing an electric current through it when it is molten or in a solution.

electromagnet A magnet which can be switched on and off by an electric current.

electron A negatively charged particle that moves around the nucleus of an atom.

electron cloud model A way of picturing electrons around an atom's nucleus. They are seen as moving randomly within cloud-like regions (also called **orbitals**).

electron configuration The number of electrons that exist in each of the shells around the nuclei of the atoms of a particular element.

electronics The use of electronic components to control the flow of a current around a circuit, making it do particular tasks.

electron shell A region (level) around an atom's nucleus in which a certain number of electrons can exist.

electroplating A method of covering an object with a thin layer of metal by electrolysis.

electrorefining A method of purifying metals using electrolysis.

element A substance made up of atoms which all have the same atomic number. It cannot be broken down by a chemical reaction to form simpler substances. See also *isotopes*.

Eureka can A container used to measure volumes of solid objects. It displaces the same volume of water as the volume of the solid put into it.

evaporation The process by which the surface molecules of a liquid escape into the air, becoming a vapour.

Ferromagnetic The term used to describe metals that can be magnetized easily.

flame test A test used to detect the presence of a particular metal by the colour of its flame.

fossil fuel A fuel such as coal, oil or natural gas, that is formed from the fossilized remains of plants or animals.

Frasch process The process by which sulphur is extracted from underground, using pressurized steam.

freezing point The temperature at which a liquid cools sufficiently to become a solid (the same temperature as the melting point of the solid).

Galvanizing A method of protecting steel from rusting by coating it with zinc.

geysers Places where hot water and steam shoot out from below the surface of the Earth.

graphite (or **plumbago**) A soft, flaky allotrope of carbon in which each atom is linked to three others in a layered formation.

group In the periodic table, a column of elements whose atoms have the same number of electrons in their outer electron shell.

Haber process The method of producing ammonia by combining hydrogen and nitrogen.

halite See *rock salt*.

halogens The five poisonous and reactive non-metallic elements that make up group VII of the periodic table. They are fluorine, chlorine, bromine, iodine and astatine.

hard water Water which contains a lot of dissolved minerals from rocks it has flowed over. **Temporary hard water** contains minerals that can be removed by boiling. The minerals in **permanent hard water** cannot.

hydrometer A device used to measure the density of a liquid.

Inner transition metals A sub-group of the transition metals. Its members share similar properties, such as high reactivity.

insulator A substance that cannot conduct electric current, or does not conduct heat well.

integrated circuit See *silicon chip*.

internal respiration The process by which animals and plants use oxygen to break down their food, producing energy and releasing carbon dioxide.

ion An atom that has become electrically charged by gaining or losing one or more electrons. A negatively charged ion is called an **anion**, a positively charged ion is called a **cation**.

isotopes Different forms of the same element. The atoms of each isotope have the same number of protons, but a different number of neutrons, in their nuclei. So isotopes of an element have the same atomic number, but different mass numbers.

Kinetic theory The idea that all substances are made up of moving particles which have varying amounts of energy, giving rise to the different states of matter.

Lanthanides (also **rare-earths** or **rare-earth metals**) A sub-group of the inner transition metals that includes lanthanum.

lava Magma which has come out onto the surface of the Earth, for instance from a volcano.

lignite (or **brown coal**) The least pure form of coal, containing 60-70% carbon.

Magma Molten rock containing dissolved gases. Solid rocks containing minerals are formed when it wells up from below the Earth's surface, cools and solidifies. When it comes onto the surface, it is known as lava.

malleable The term used to describe metals that can be shaped by hammering.

mass The amount of matter contained in an object.

mass number The total number of protons and neutrons in the nucleus of an atom. The mass number of two atoms of the same element may be different, because they may be different isotopes.

mass spectrometer A device used to help identify atoms by sorting them by mass.

melting point The temperature at which a substance turns from a solid into a liquid (the same temperature as the freezing point of the liquid).

metalloids See *semi-metals*.

metallurgy The study of metals and their extraction.

metals Substances which make up three-quarters of all known elements. They are mostly shiny, solid at room temperature, have high melting points, and are good conductors of electricity and heat.

minerals The naturally occurring single and combined elements of which rocks are made.

mining The removal of minerals from the ground.

Mohs scale A scale by which the hardness of minerals is measured.

molecule The smallest particle of an element or compound that exists on its own and keeps its properties.

Nanotube A specially engineered microscopic fibre produced from graphite.

native elements Minerals consisting of a single element, e.g. gold.

neutron A subatomic particle with no electric charge. Neutrons form part of the nuclei of every atom (except those of hydrogen).

noble gases The six highly unreactive elements (all gases) present in the atmosphere which together form group VIII of the periodic table. They are helium, neon, argon, krypton, xenon and radon. The atoms of a seventh member of group VIII, ununoctium, can only be produced for fractions of seconds. It is not normally considered as a noble gas.

noble metal A metal, such as gold, that can be found naturally in a pure state.

non-metals Elements that are usually non-shiny, poor conductors, with low melting and boiling points. Eleven of the 16 known non-metals are gases at room temperature, four are solids and one (bromine) is a liquid.

nucleus The core section of an atom that contains protons and (except hydrogen) neutrons.

Orbital See *electron cloud model*.

ore A mineral compound from which a metal can be extracted.

organic compound A compound that contains the element carbon.

oxide A compound of oxygen and another element.

oxygen (O_2) A gas present in the Earth's atmosphere which is vital for life. It is also the most common element in the Earth's crust, found combined with other elements as oxides.

Particle accelerator A machine which accelerates charged subatomic particles to a great speed, in order that new particles produced by their collisions may be studied.

period A set of elements which have electrons in the same number of electron shells, shown as a row in the periodic table.

periodic table A systematic arrangement of the elements in order of increasing atomic number.

photon See *quantum theory*.

photosynthesis The process by which plants use energy from sunlight to power the conversion of water and carbon dioxide into carbohydrates.

physical states See *states of matter*.

plastic The term used to describe a substance which does not return to its original shape after stretching, but instead holds a new shape. See also *elastic*.

plumbago See *graphite*.

poor metals A group of nine metals, including aluminium and lead. They are mostly quite soft, and are usually combined with other substances to make alloys.

pressure The force exerted over a given area by a solid, liquid or gas.

proton A positively charged subatomic particle. Protons form part of the nucleus of every atom.

Quantum theory The idea that energy comes in tiny "packets", called **quanta**. It helps to explain the properties of electrons and the relationship of energy to matter. Quanta of electromagnetic radiation, such as light, are called photons.

quarks Particles which are believed to make up protons and neutrons.

Radioactive rare earths See *actinides*.

radioactivity The release of energy from the nuclei of unstable atoms. The energy, in the form of radiation, can be dangerous in large quantities.

radioisotope A radioactive isotope.

rare earths See *lanthanides*.

reactivity The tendency of a substance to react with other substances.

reactivity series A list of elements, usually metals, arranged in order of how easily they react with other substances.

recycling Making materials, such as metals, reusable by treating them in various ways.

red phosphorus A dark red, powdery allotrope of phosphorus, used to make matches.

reduction A chemical reaction in which a substance loses oxygen, or gains hydrogen or electrons. The opposite is **oxidation**, and the two processes normally occur together.

relative atomic mass The average mass number of the atoms in an exactly measured sample of an element (the mass numbers of the atoms may differ due to the presence of isotopes).

relative density A substance's density in relation to the density of water.

rhombic sulphur The commonest allotrope of sulphur, with closely fitting molecules.

rock salt (or **halite**) The mineral form of common salt (sodium chloride).

rust Iron oxide that forms on the surface of iron, or an iron alloy, due to corrosion. It gradually flakes off, causing the iron to deteriorate.

Sacrificial metal A metal used to coat a less reactive metal, protecting it by corroding first.

semiconductor A type of material, usually a semi-metal, that acts as a conductor or as an insulator depending on its temperature.

semi-metals (or **metalloids**) Elements which share some of the properties of metals and non-metals, and which can, depending on their temperature, be either conductors or insulators. They are all solids at room temperature. See also *semiconductor*.

shell See *electron shell*.

silicon chip (also **integrated circuit** or **chip**) A tiny piece of silicon with a complete electronic circuit etched onto it.

slag Impurities present in iron ore, left over as waste after smelting.

smelting The process of extracting a metal, usually iron, from its ore by heating to high temperatures, and reducing the ore.

solution A mixture that consists of a substance dissolved in a liquid.

space-filling model A way of representing molecules in which chemically bonded atoms are shown as balls clinging together.

stainless steel An alloy of steel and chromium that is both strong and resistant to corrosion.

standard pressure See *atmospheric pressure*.

states of matter (or **physical states**) The different forms in which a substance can exist. The three basic states are solid, liquid and gas.

subatomic particles Particles smaller than an atom, especially those of which atoms are made: protons, electrons and neutrons.

sublimation A change from solid to gas, or gas to solid, without going through liquid form.

superalloy An extremely strong, durable alloy that usually contains nickel, iron or cobalt.

surface tension The force of attraction that pulls together the molecules on the surface of a liquid.

synthetic The term describing compound materials that are made artificially by chemical reactions in a factory.

Transistor An electronic component which acts as a switch by using a small current to control a larger one.

transition metals The largest group of metals, mostly hard and tough in nature, with high melting points.

Volume The amount of space a substance occupies.

vulcanization A process used to strengthen rubber by heating it with sulphur.

Weight A measure of the strength of the pull of gravity on an object.

white phosphorus The most reactive allotrope of phosphorus, a poisonous white solid that ignites in air.

INDEX

You will find the main explanations of terms in the index on the pages shown in bold type. It may be useful to look at the other pages for further information.

ACKNOWLEDGEMENTS

PHOTO CREDITS
(t = top, m = middle, b = bottom, l = left, r = right)

Corbis: **1** Eye Ubiquitous; **2-3** Science Pictures Ltd.; **10** (bl) Jim Sugar Photography; **12-13** (main) Digital Art; **14-15** W. Perry Conway; **16** (tl) Fukuhara Inc; **17** (m) Keren Su; **20-21** Roger Ressmeyer; **22** (bl) Jim Zuckerman; **24-25** Ric Ergenbright; **28-29** Buddy Mays; **30** (tr) Phil Schermeister; **32** Dan Guravich; **34-35** Dean Conger; **38-39** Roger Ressmeyer; **40-41** (main) Charles E. Rotkin; **41** (tr) Roger Ressmeyer; **43** (tr) James L. Amos; **46-47** (main) Charles O'Rear; **50-51** (main) Charles O'Rear; **53** (main) Owen Franken.
© **Digital Vision**: 4-5; 6-7;**17** (tm), (b); **19** (l); **20** (tr); **22-23**; **23** (m); **30** (br); **31**; **33** (ml); **35** (mr); **36** (tr); **36-37**; **39** (tr), (m), (mr); **42** (bm); **42-43**; **44** (t), (b); **46** (l); **50** (bl); **51** (tl); **54-55**.
Science Photo Library cover Sinclair Stammers; **NASA 49** (bm)
Crown copyright Historic Royal Palaces 48 (Reproduced by permission of Historic Royal Palaces under licence from the controller of Her Majesty's Stationery Office);
Lawson Mardon Star Ltd, Bridgnorth 22 (bm); **39** (l); **Robert M. Reed 25** (bm);
Ullstein Bilderdienst/Max Machon 45 (bm); **www.trekbikes.com 50** (m)

ILLUSTRATORS
Simone Abel, Sophie Allington, Rex Archer, Paul Bambrick, Jeremy Banks, Andrew Beckett, Joyce Bee, Stephen Bennett, Roland Berry, Gary Bines, Isabel Bowring, Trevor Boyer, John Brettoner, Peter Bull, Hilary Burn, Andy Burton, Terry Callcut, Kuo Kang Chen, Stephen Conlin, Sydney Cornfield, Dan Courtney, Steve Cross, Gordon Davies, Peter Dennis, Richard Draper, Brin Edwards, Sandra Fernandez, Denise Finney, John Francis, Mark Franklin, Nigel Frey, Giacinto Gaudenzi, Peter Geissler, Nick Gibbard, William Giles, David Goldston, Peter Goodwin, Jeremy Gower, Teri Gower, Terry Hadler, Bob Hersey, Nicholas Hewetson, Christine Howes, Inklink Firenze, Ian Jackson, Karen Johnson, Richard Johnson, Elaine Keenan, Aziz Khan, Stephen Kirk, Richard Lewington, Brian Lewis, Jason Lewis, Steve Lings, Rachel Lockwood, Kevin Lyles, Chris Lyon, Kevin Maddison, Janos Marffy, Andy Martin, Josephine Martin, Peter Massey, Rob McCaig, Joseph McEwan, David McGrail, Malcolm McGregor, Christina McInerney, Caroline McLean, Dee McLean, Annabel Milne, Sean Milne, Robert Morton, Louise Nevet, Martin Newton, Louise Nixon, Steve Page, Justine Peek, Mick Posen, Russell Punter, Barry Raynor, Mark Roberts, Andrew Robinson, Michael Roffe, Michelle Ross, Michael Saunders, John Scorey, John Shackell, Chris Shields, David Slinn, Guy Smith, Peter Stebbing, Robert Walster, Craig Warwick, Ross Watton, Phil Weare, Hans Wiborg-Jenssen, Sean Wilkinson, Ann Winterbottom, Gerald Wood, David Wright.

Every effort has been made to trace the copyright holders of the material in this book. If any rights have been omitted, the publishers offer to rectify this in any future edition, following notification.